W9-BWH-514

The Night the
Martians
Landed

**Just the Facts
(Plus the Rumors)
About Invaders from Mars**

The Night the Martians Landed

Just the Facts
(Plus the Rumors)
About Invaders from Mars

by Kathleen Krull

illustrations by
Christopher Santoro

HarperCollins*Publishers*

Library of Congress Cataloging-in-Publication Data is
available.

ISBN 0-688-172474

Typography by Amy Ryan

❖

First edition

To Andy Hill and his parents,
Donna and Ned
-K.K.

For Bud the radio man
-C.S.

They say something incredible happened in Grovers Mill, New Jersey. The date was October 30, 1938. Aliens were involved.

Many stories are told about that night. The book you are holding will reveal:

- **the facts**

- **some of the rumors**

The night before Halloween 1938 was just another sleepy Sunday evening. A little fog blurred the east coast, but nothing serious. In a typical American home, the mom might have been sticking supper leftovers in the icebox, while the dad carved the jack-o'-lantern. Teens would be plotting Halloween pranks or out for a Sunday drive in the family Ford or Chrysler. Younger kids were perfecting costumes for their big night of trick-or-treating.

In the America of 1938, no one had a TV. Plenty of people still didn't have phones, cars, or indoor plumbing. But nearly everyone had a radio. That night, an estimated six million Americans gathered around their "magic boxes."

In 1909, Italian scientist Guglielmo Marconi shared a Nobel Prize in physics for developing wireless telegraphy, or radio. This new technology played a key role in World War I, and, in 1920, radio broadcasting became available to the public.

Most radios were tuned to NBC. The hugely popular ventriloquist Edgar Bergen was trading jokes with his puppet, Charlie McCarthy. But people would switch stations if they got bored, and there were all sorts of other things to listen to.

In the CBS radio studio in New York City, a young actor soothed his throat with pineapple juice. Orson Welles and the Mercury Theatre Players were about to perform their own version of *The War of the Worlds*, an old science-fiction novel by H. G. Wells.

Even though this was their seventeenth show, the Mercury Theatre hadn't really caught on with audiences. They had no commercial sponsor. Some of the actors thought tonight's script was silly and feared they were about to make fools of themselves. Standing in front of their microphones, a few still argued for performing *Lorna Doone,* a classic romantic adventure, instead.

Despite the similarity of their last names, H. G. Wells and Orson Welles were not related.

But at 8 P.M. eastern time, the Mercury Theatre broadcast "The War of the Worlds" streamed live into radios all over America.

The show began as a pleasant little evening of music from a swanky hotel ballroom. A conductor named Ramón Raquello and his orchestra played vaguely Spanish music.

Suddenly an announcer cut in: "Ladies and gentlemen, we interrupt our program of dance music to bring you a special bulletin . . ."

He went on to say that a "huge, flaming object" had crashed on a farm in New Jersey. The impact was said to be as intense as an earthquake. Was it a meteorite?

As a boy in Kenosha, Wisconsin, Orson Welles (1915–1985) won praise for his magnificent voice and acting talent. He first read *The War of the Worlds* in comic book installments at age twelve. By 1938, he was twenty-three, a supremely self-confident boy genius. Already, on a radio show called *The Shadow,* his voice gave kids shivers when he laughed wickedly and said, "The Shadow knows ..."

The music came back. But soon a perky reporter named Carl Phillips began interrupting with bulletins from Grovers Mill, a tiny New Jersey town.

Phillips tried to interview Mr.

Wilmuth, the owner of the farm where this mysterious object had landed. Mr. Wilmuth was mumbly, so Phillips went back to painting word pictures.

The object was not a meteorite but a large yellowish cylinder. Creepy sounds came from the pit where it had landed.

The top of the cylinder lifted and a head wiggled out. A head with tentacles.

Phillips shrieked. "Ladies and gentlemen," he sobbed, "this is the most terrifying thing I have ever witnessed. . . . There, I can see the thing's body. It's large, large as a bear and it glistens like wet leather. But that face . . . The eyes are black and gleam like a serpent. The mouth is V-shaped with saliva dripping from its rimless lips that seem to quiver and pulsate. . . ."

Herbert George Wells (1866–1946) lived in England. He started out as a science teacher, then helped to invent a new type of literature now known as science fiction. His novels *The Time Machine* and *The Invisible Man* were very successful, selling more than *The War of the Worlds* (1898). He was known as "the man who invented tomorrow," but by 1938 his reputation was slipping due to his scandalous love life.

The cylinder was obviously some kind of spaceship. Phillips fought to keep his cool. His stammering was overwhelmed by sounds of angry police and confused, frightened bystanders.

Phillips signed off to find a safer position so he could continue reporting.

A studio announcer broke in: "We are bringing you an eyewitness account of what's happening on the Wilmuth farm, Grovers Mill, New Jersey."

Unsure of whether he was still on the air, Carl Phillips continued talking . . . but now the monster was blasting the police and onlookers with a strange weapon made of fire!

The pace of his reporting sped up until Phillips was babbling. In the background, terrified human screams and moans from the monster merged into a hair-raising roar.

Then came the sound of nothing. Dead air.

After a minute, various people spoke. Princeton University, conveniently close to Grovers Mill, was the source for expert opinions. A Professor Pierson, an eyewitness to the horrible events, called the mystery weapon a deadly heat-ray. Other scientists discussed what they knew of outer space.

The Secretary of the Interior came on to ask Americans to stay calm. Military officers discussed strategy.

At least forty people were found dead. One of the charred bodies was identified as Carl Phillips.

Yet another announcer came on: "Those strange beings who landed in the Jersey farmlands tonight are the vanguard of an invading army from the planet Mars."

In other words, Martians had landed.

There had never been any concrete evidence that Martians exist. But if any planet could harbor life, astronomers have thought it would be Mars, the one most like Earth. A few years before Wells wrote *The War of the Worlds,* Mars came unusually close to Earth. Newspapers were packed with observations that fired up Wells's brain. To give his story conflict, he created a war between humans and aliens. To make it even scarier, he wrote in a documentary style, tying events to real places in England. He even described Martians destroying places he didn't like, "killing my neighbors in painful and eccentric ways."

The show went on just as a real crisis might on the radio, with bulletins, public announcements, and on-the-scene reports.

The Martian retreated into its pit. But it came back—this time encased in a three-legged machine as tall as a skyscraper.

Seven thousand soldiers of the New Jersey National Guard had been called out. The Martian killed almost all of them. Instantly. Then it began marching east across the state of New Jersey.

Other Martians arrived. They joined the march, blasting people and communication lines with their heat-rays and spraying a poisonous black gas.

The U.S. Army mobilized bomber planes to attack, but they were no match for the Martians' weapons. It was announced that gas masks were useless against the Martian spray.

It was shocking to imagine, but it was obvious that the alien intelligence was superior to ours.

Now the Martians were heading for New York City, killing everyone in their path.

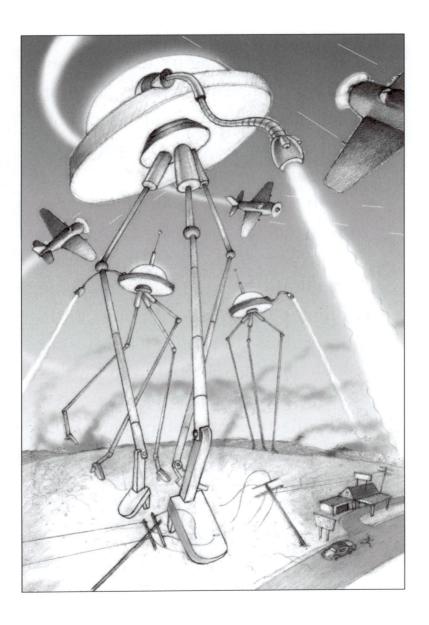

Bells began clanging to warn New Yorkers to get out. Five Martian death machines were on their way, spraying the poison gas, making a dreadful *swish* sound.

Then a lonely, nameless announcer spoke from the roof of the CBS building in New York City. He reported that all streets were jammed. Three million people were driving north, the bridges to Long Island were hopelessly packed, and overcrowded boats were pulling out from New York's harbor. Amid the roar of the crowd was the sound of people singing hymns.

"All communication with Jersey shore closed ten minutes ago," the announcer said numbly. "No more defenses. Our army wiped out . . . artillery, air force, everything wiped out."

Then he delivered the worst news of all: Martian spaceships were now landing all over the country. There was one outside Buffalo, one in Chicago, another in St. Louis . . .

There was no escape.

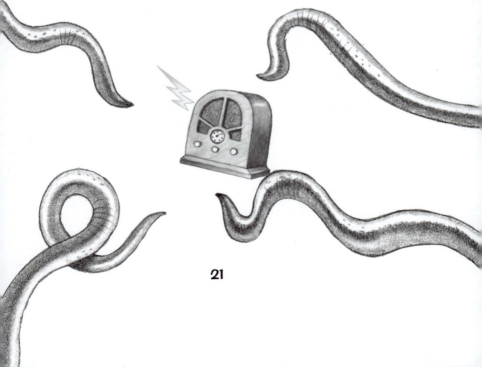

From the roof, the announcer could actually see the first of the Martian death machines, "wading the Hudson like a man wading through a brook." Soon five great shapes were silhouetted against the night sky: "Now they're lifting their metal hands. This is the end now. Smoke comes out . . . black smoke, drifting over the city."

Thousands of people hurled themselves into the East River, "dropping in like rats."

The smoke reached Times Square: "People trying to run away from it, but it's no use. They're falling like flies. Now the smoke's crossing Sixth Avenue . . . Fifth Avenue . . . one hundred yards away . . . it's fifty feet. . . ."

The sound of a body falling.

It was, it appeared, the end of the world.

Why were these Martians so mean? This goes back to a hypothesis made by American astronomer Percival Lowell in 1895. Lowell believed that the existence of "canals" on Mars meant that it once had water that could have supported life. H. G. Wells knew Lowell's work and came up with the idea of Mars as a dying planet with an advanced civilization that was desperate to find a new place to live.

Next an announcer came on for a CBS station identification, adding, "The performance will continue after a brief intermission." This was one of three times during the broadcast when it was clearly stated that what people were hearing was a play.

After the break, Orson Welles went on the air, speaking in the shell-shocked voice of Princeton's Professor Pierson as he wandered around. Eventually he came to Central Park in New York, where he discovered the "corpses" of nineteen Martian machines.

Heavily armed as they were, the Martians had forgotten one thing: to build up their resistance to bacteria.

It was this simplest of Earth's organisms that killed them. Pierson reveals that the human race has been saved, and so the world goes on.

Now Orson Welles came on as himself. This show was, he said, "the Mercury Theatre's own radio version of dressing up in a sheet and jumping out of a bush and saying Boo!"

It was over. The whole "The War of the Worlds" broadcast had taken about forty-five minutes. With no company sponsoring the Mercury Theatre, there had been no break for commercials.

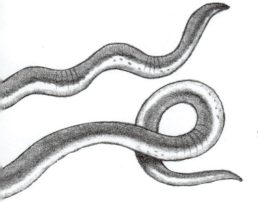

26

H. G. Wells was trying to write a page-turner, the most thrilling story possible. But he also had serious points to make. One was that humans were horribly destructive—they exterminated animals and even members of their own species. In *The War of the Worlds*, he wanted to show powerful humans becoming powerless—so that they would develop compassion.

About ten minutes into the broadcast, however, the night had taken a wrong turn.

Telephone switchboards lit up all over the country. CBS, local radio stations, state National Guard armories, and hospitals—all were flooded with calls. *The New York Times* received 875 calls. Thousands of them came in to the Newark police headquarters in New Jersey.

The part about "The War of the Worlds" broadcast being a play? Certain people had missed it. They thought that Earth was being invaded by Martians—for real.

At first the calls were from anxious relatives of New Jersey residents.

Then people were calling friends and family to say good-bye. Everyone was crying. National Guard members called to report for duty. Hundreds of doctors and nurses called hospitals to volunteer their services. Grocery store owners asked where to send food for the "victims." The governor of Pennsylvania offered troops to help stop the "invasion." Electric companies received scores of pleas to kill lights so that cities would be hidden from the "enemy."

People ran outside to look at the sky. Many covered their faces with wet towels for protection against the "poison gas." Others hid in cellars, hoping the gas would blow over them.

Some people fled. They packed their stuff and went to parks or more rural areas, raiding grocery stores on their way. College students tried to get home to their families. Some people had no destination. Everyone was driving recklessly, ignoring signs, breaking speed records, and causing traffic jams.

Some people froze, holding hands and waiting in dread for the monsters. Some raided their iceboxes to eat Sunday dinner leftovers (no point in wasting them).

Others vomited and became ill. One New Jersey hospital treated fifteen people for shock and hysteria.

The news spread to those who weren't listening to the radio. Frantic moviegoers ran out of theaters, and people poured out of bars. Sunday evening church services were interrupted and turned into what *The New York Times* called "'end of the world' prayer meetings."

At a wedding reception in Manhattan, everyone took to the streets, despite the bride's pleas to stay.

Those who had them reached for their guns and began forming neighborhood patrols.

In Hollywood, gossips claimed that the famous actor John Barrymore let his ten Great Danes outside, shouting, "The world is finished, fend for yourselves!"

One despairing woman in Pennsylvania was about to swallow poison when her husband found her.

People blamed coincidences on the Martians. Any flickering of electricity meant that Martians were cutting power lines. That eerie light in the house across the street came from a monster.

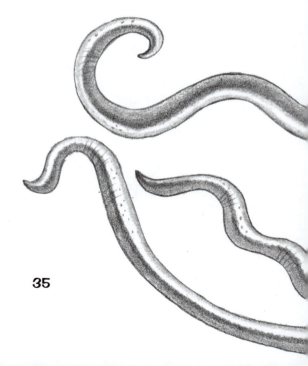

Another one of Wells's "messages" was that, in a crisis, all people will lose their civilized ways and become savages. And, indeed, civilized behavior did tend to vanish the night this version of Wells's story was broadcast.

Strangest of all were reports con-
firming specific details of the "invasion." People said they were being
choked by the gas. Some said they
could see smoke drifting over New
York and "Martians on their giant
machines poised on the Jersey
Palisades." Witnesses reported a red
glow against the night sky, machine-
gun fire, and the *swish* sound of
aliens.

None of these things were real. Nor
were Ramón Raquello, Carl Phillips,
Mr. Wilmuth, Professor Pierson—all
were made up by Howard Koch, who
adapted Wells's novel for the
Mercury Theatre.

But Grovers Mill? That was a real
place in New Jersey. So the alarm,

naturally, was most intense there. Early on, two real Princeton professors took their geology tools and searched for the "meteorite." Farmers with shotguns roamed the countryside and even fired shots at a tall water tower with metal legs—so easy to mistake for a Martian. The local fire chief spent all night chasing down reports of fires set off in the woods by Martian heat-rays. A hundred New Jersey state troopers—real ones—were sent in to keep the peace.

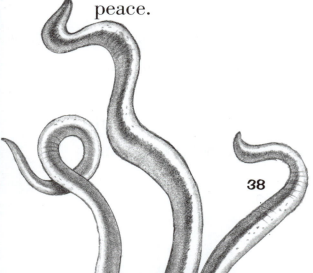

Howard Koch, Mercury Theatre's writer, wanted to add spice to the story by changing H. G. Wells's locale of Victorian England to real places in 1938 New Jersey. He picked Grovers Mill by closing his eyes and pointing his pencil on a road map.

Back at the CBS studio, Orson Welles was in trouble. New York City police officers—real ones—crowded outside the glass-enclosed control room. By the end of the broadcast, at

9 P.M., they were ready to arrest him. The Federal Communications Commission was threatening an investigation. People were already planning to file lawsuits (reported by the newspapers as eventually totaling $12 million).

Leaving Welles behind, the other actors scurried out the back door.

Just one problem—no one could find a law that Welles had actually broken.

Around the country, the panic died down during the night. Every radio station reassured Americans that there was no cause for alarm, explaining that it had all been make-believe.

On Monday, the next day, CBS ordered Welles to apologize. The station also promised never again to use a fake news broadcast that had the potential to alarm.

The best Welles could do for an apology was to say, "Radio is new and we are learning about the effect it has on people." At Monday's press conference, he beamed at reporters and photographers and claimed to be "shocked" that anyone could have taken the show as fact.

For weeks, the "Panic Broadcast," as it came to be known, dominated news around the world. Angry reactions changed to giggles at listeners who'd been so gullible. The lawsuits—blaming miscarriages, heart attacks, other injuries and damages on the broadcast—went away or were dismissed.

Amazingly enough, in all the chaos, no one had died. But study of that night went on for years. How could so many have confused entertainment for reality? How could they ignore the way the broadcast squished weeks of activity into forty-five minutes? How did they miss all three announcements that this was a play? And what about the basic fact that we don't even know if Martians exist?

Were people really that stupid?

Not necessarily. For one thing, the Mercury Theatre did a great job. The sound effects were chillingly real, and all the actors *sounded* so trustworthy. Orson Welles was one of the best actors alive—when he said something, you simply believed it.

The actor who played the Secretary of the Interior deliberately tried to imitate President Franklin Delano Roosevelt, whose voice was familiar. On the radio in real life, FDR was giving friendly "fireside chats" to keep spirits up during the horrendous Great Depression that began in 1929.

The actor who played the doomed Carl Phillips imitated another real person.

Only seventeen months earlier, an eyewitness reporter had been describing the routine landing of the zeppelin *Hindenburg*, at Lakehurst, New Jersey, when the airship exploded, killing thirty-six passengers and crew. It was the first disaster in history to be broadcast live. The shocked reporter fought to remain coherent, and his sobbing, second-by-second description became world famous.

The actor portraying Carl Phillips listened to the Hindenburg recording over and over. The emotion, the stammering, and even his pace reminded many people of the broadcast of the *Hindenburg* disaster—and they took it as real.

Using real places, such as Grovers Mill and New York City, added some credibility. If the English locations had been used, listeners would have been less apt to panic and may have even caught on much quicker.

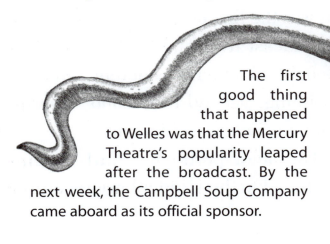

The first good thing that happened to Welles was that the Mercury Theatre's popularity leaped after the broadcast. By the next week, the Campbell Soup Company came aboard as its official sponsor.

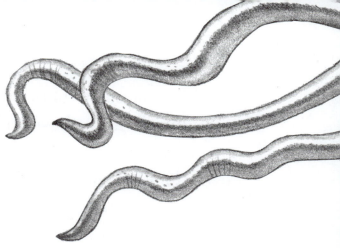

Meanwhile, over in England, H. G. Wells was outraged. He issued a statement that the dramatization was made with "a liberty that amounts to a complete rewriting and made the novel an entirely different story." He went on to say that he had not given permission for alterations which might lead to the belief that Martians had really landed.

In their defense, many Americans hadn't heard the whole broadcast. They tuned in at various points and heard fragments. Others got the news secondhand, from those they had no reason to doubt. Nothing spreads faster than bad news.

There was, of course, no TV to confirm or deny the story, no Internet, no way of checking. Some who flipped the dial and heard nothing about Martians on other stations caught on, but others didn't. They assumed CBS had the exclusive story—or that Martians had taken control of the radio waves.

In many people's minds, radio already had a connection to Mars. Some believed that static and other interference was caused by competing Martian radio signals. Even Marconi, inventor of the radio, assumed that he was receiving messages from Mars.

In 1938, thoughts of war and invasion weren't all that far-fetched. World War I, with its scary new weapons of quick-killing poison gas and machine guns, had ended only twenty years earlier. Suspense about a second world war was mounting toward a breaking point, possibly with even more deadly weapons to come.

A month before the broadcast, Britain, Germany, Italy, and France had signed the Munich Pact, which appeased Hitler—for the time being. America's role in the war brewing in Europe was unknown, but people were twitchy. "We interrupt this broadcast" was becoming all too familiar.

Some listeners believed that an invasion *was* taking place that night—by Germans or Japanese. The announcers had simply been mistaken about the Martian part.

On December 7, 1941, when Japanese planes bombed Pearl Harbor, some people assumed the initial radio reports were fake, an Orson Welles kind of hoax.

In 1940, a real Princeton University expert named Hadley Cantril published a scholarly study of that night. According to Dr. Cantril, approximately six million people in the United States heard the broadcast. More than one million took it seriously. People who had the most years of education and the most knowledge of the world were the least likely to have been fooled.

The main reason that the others panicked? Insecurity. The Great Depression had rocked Americans with the sudden loss of jobs, farms, and businesses. Some didn't know what to believe anymore. Especially to those listeners already obsessed with end-of-the-world prophecies, the broadcast rang true.

Also, the world was changing fast, especially in science and technology, and things that had seemed impossible—airplanes, electricity, radio itself—were suddenly possible. An alien invasion . . . well, why not?

Articles pointed out that age could have been a factor in the panic. Somehow, many younger listeners intuitively understood that "The War of the Worlds" broadcast was a fantasy and said they wouldn't have panicked if their parents hadn't.

Dr. Cantril and others pointed out that something in human nature makes us want to believe we are not alone in the universe. Ever since Percival Lowell and the earliest claims about Martian life, studies have shown that such claims are accepted by most of the public— even when they are not accepted by most scientists and astronomers.

Also, the idea that these aliens were unfriendly somehow made more sense than if they had just wanted a cup of coffee. Outer space is unknown territory, and most people's reaction to the unknown is fear. Radio is actually better for fright than TV—the pictures in your mind are scarier than anything anyone else can show you. And fear produces a body chemical called adrenaline, which in times of stress makes it difficult to think clearly.

Orson Welles's "The War of the Worlds" played masterfully to our fear of the unknown. Even today it remains the most famous story about

Martians. It gave people nightmares and created our image of Martians as hideous creatures with giant brains. It inspired TV shows such as *Star Trek*, comic books, computer games, and too many invasion movies to list.

The following are just a few of the movies about alien invasion: *Independence Day*, *Mars Attacks!*, and dozens of 1950s sci-fi movies, including *I Married a Monster from Outer Space*, *Invasion of the Body Snatchers*, *The Day the Earth Stood Still*, and *Plan 9 from Outer Space* (considered by some to be the worst movie ever made).

Over time, the reported number of those who actually panicked has shrunk from Dr. Cantril's original one million estimate. (Of course, anyone who was tricked then would probably deny it now.)

As the years went by, witnesses became more apt to say the broadcast was "the thrill of a lifetime"—like an amusement park ride. Some people told Orson Welles they found it more funny than scary. They fondly recalled it as "the biggest Halloween prank of all time."

Some decided that the newspapers—which hated radio for taking away their readers—had exaggerated the fuss.

Some even wondered if the idea of a huge scare was a hoax in itself. Could the government have deliberately created the panic in the first place, just so it could have an excuse later to clamp down on *real* information about aliens?

Orson Welles kept changing his mind about whether the panic surprised him. Once he admitted that "we expected a lunatic fringe but we didn't know it would go all across the country." Later he said he did want to shake people up—teach them a lesson about not believing everything they heard.

Thanks to the 1958 creation of the National Aeronautics and Space Administration (NASA), we got to know Mars better. In 1965, a robotic spacecraft came within six thousand miles of Mars and took twenty-two pictures—discovering more than astronomers had learned in all the previous years put together. We saw the pictures on TV (which began regular broadcasts in 1951). Conclusion: no canals, no life.

In 1971, another space probe, *Mariner 9*, was launched, which took more than seven thousand pictures. Conclusion this time: no life, but some evidence that Mars once had flowing water—so it may have *had* life.

Between 1975 and 1980, Viking

probes landed right on Mars and beamed back scenery. In a bone-dry desert, with temperatures one hundred degrees below zero and lethal radiation from the sun, scientists concluded that Mars had fascinating geography. But there was no proof of life.

Disappointment slowed the pace of discoveries. In 1984, an American geologist named Roberta Score found what appeared to be a greenish rock near the South Pole. It turned out to be a meteorite, or a chunk, of Mars. It had spent sixteen million years wandering the solar system, hitting Antarctica thirteen thousand years ago. Scientific testing of this rock offered likely but not definite evidence that Mars once had primitive life.

People got excited again, and NASA's unmanned *Pathfinder* landed on Mars in 1997. That day there were one hundred million hits on the mission's website—now the Internet is the way we find out what's going on.

More Martian probes are scheduled by NASA and by European and Asian agencies. Sooner or later, humans will be aboard—it's more likely that humans will invade Mars than the other way around. Scientists have big plans: exploration, colonization, and the possible solution to global warming and other Earth problems. Perhaps, in your lifetime, *you* will make the six-month trip.

The Panic Broadcast did seem to teach Americans to be more skeptical, less trusting of "official" voices. It has been called "the most socially significant broadcast ever."

It certainly helped everyone who was in it. Orson Welles went to Hollywood, where he was given big contracts to make movies. Many consider his *Citizen Kane* (1941) to be the best movie of all time. Howard Koch, Mercury Theatre's writer, also moved to Hollywood, where he wrote *Casablanca* (1942), among many other movies.

Over the years, though, the two hundred or so residents of Grovers Mill got sick of being interviewed. Still, in 1988, the fiftieth anniversary of the broadcast, the town threw a grand celebration. The many activities included the burying of a time capsule to be opened in 2038.

Today the "invaders" of Grovers Mill are sightseers. You can visit the water tower that looked like a Martian and the farm where the spaceship "crashed." Mr. Wilmuth was a made-up character, but everyone has decided a real farm owned by Mr. Wilson was the spot.

And today Mars is always in the news. (For the very latest, see the websites in the sources section at the end of this book). Finding even a tiny bit of life there would rank as one of the most amazing discoveries of all time.

H. G. Wells changed his mind about Orson Welles when sales of his novel perked up. The two met in 1940—in a live radio interview—in which H. G. referred to the broadcast as "this sensational Halloween panic spree" by his "delightful little namesake."

Orson Welles's Halloween "Boo!" stands as a unique night in American history: All sorts of people from all over the country were seriously disturbed by something that wasn't true.

It's easy to feel superior. But a fake story—spread via a new invention such as the Internet—could just as well terrorize today. (Actually, nearly every October, some group performs a version of "The War of the Worlds"—in Quito, Ecuador; Buffalo, New York; Portugal; Providence, Rhode Island; and elsewhere—and people sometimes panic all over again.)

In December 1999, millions freaked at untrustworthy rumors about the Y2K change of the millennium. They hoarded food and supplies, stockpiled cash, bought weapons, and even dug bunkers to hide in—in case January 2000 meant the end of the world. And all this ruckus was caused by people believing what they heard.

Hoaxes spread like wildfire on the Internet every day, and people fall for them. It's human nature to believe what we read or hear. No matter how high-tech we become, how cool we think we are, we can still be fooled.

Scientists may say Martians don't exist, but this has not stopped rumors that they do. Some people believe the government could be covering up. And why?

To avoid, at all costs, a panic like the night the Martians landed.

Sources

Books

Bulgatz, Joseph. *Ponzi Schemes, Invaders from Mars and More Extraordinary Popular Delusions and the Madness of Crowds.* New York: Harmony Books, 1992.

Cantril, Hadley. *The Invasion from Mars: A Study in the Psychology of Panic.* Princeton: Princeton University Press, 1940.

Feeler, Fred. *Media Hoaxes.* Ames: Iowa State University Press, 1989.

Fradin, Dennis Brindell. *Is There Life on Mars?* New York: Margaret McElderry, 1999.

Holmstein, Brian, and Alex Lubertozzi, editors. *The Complete War of the Worlds: Mars' Invasion of Earth from H. G. Wells to Orson Welles.* Naperville, IL: Sourcebooks, Inc., 2001.

Koch, Howard. *The Panic Broadcast: Portrait of an Event.* Boston: Little, Brown, 1970.

Websites

Exploring Mars (for young readers)—www.exploringmars.com/

NASA Official Mars Exploration Website—mars.jpl.nasa.gov/

The Estate of Orson Welles—www.bway.net/~nipper/home.html

The H. G. Wells Society—www.hgwellsusa.50megs.com

The Official Grovers Mill War of
the Worlds website (includes the
broadcast)—www.waroftheworlds.org/
H. G. Wells's *The War of the
Worlds* online (among other sites)—
www.fourmilab.ch/etexts/www/war
worlds/warw.html
Mars Orbiter Camera Image
Gallery (pictures from NASA's Mars
Global Surveyor)—
www.msss.com/moc_gallery/
The Mars Society—
www.marssociety.org/
The Mercury Theatre on the Air
(includes the broadcast)—
www.unknown.nu/mercury
Complete Mercury Theatre script,
History of American Broadcasting—
members.aol.com/jeff1070/script.html

Newspaper accounts
of the broadcast—
members.aol.com/jeff1070/wotw.html
Search for Extraterrestrial
Intelligence (SETI) Institute—
www.seti.org
Urban Legends Reference Pages
(includes Internet hoaxes)—
www.snopes.com/

TV Shows

"Martian Mania: The True Story of
the *War of the Worlds*," Sci-Fi
Channel documentary, October 30,
1998, hosted by James Cameron.

If you like aliens
. . . read on!

The night of June 13, 1947, was like no other night ever. A bizarre event took place in the desert outside the little town of Roswell, New Mexico.

Out of that forever-starry sky, an object fell to the ground.

On June 14, eight-year-old Vernon Brazel woke up at dawn. All day long, he helped out with chores on his dad's sprawling sheep ranch. His dad, W. W. Brazel, nicknamed Mac, barreled his truck right over the desert sand. Their ranch was so lonely that no roads led to it.

In the late afternoon, Vernon spotted

something in the distance. Something gleaming on the ground. What was it?

But Mac wouldn't stop the truck. He was too busy with the daily rounds of the ranch to even pay Vernon much attention.

That night, over a dinner of cold pork and beans and crackers, Mac mentioned Vernon's excitement to Mrs. Brazel. Vernon's fourteen-year-old sister, Bessie, got excited, too. It didn't really occur to anyone in the family to call the police.

Even if they had wanted to, the Brazels didn't have a phone.

Over the next three weeks, Vernon and Bessie Brazel almost went crazy. They were itching to go back and explore what Vernon had seen.

Finally, on the Fourth of July, Mac took a day off. He drove his family back out into the bleak desert. Vernon pointed the way.

Soon they glimpsed something in the middle of nowhere, some stuff that seemed to have dropped right out of the sky. Vernon and Bessie hopped out and raced around to gather up strange silvery scraps. The mystery material was etched with unearthly writing in pink and purple. Bessie and Vernon tried to make sense of it, gave up, then stuffed the material into sacks that once contained food for the sheep. Altogether the sacks weighed about five pounds.

If you'd like to find out what Vernon and Bessie found, read

WHAT REALLY HAPPENED IN ROSWELL? *Just the Facts (Plus The Rumors) About UFOs and Aliens* by Kathleen Krull, with illustrations by Christopher Santoro.

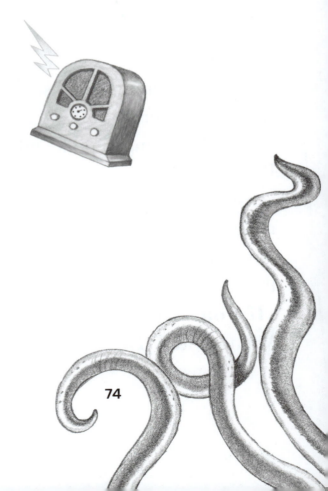